Lata Mangeshkar
India's Nightingale
Learn Hindi Through Stories

Nicole Herbert Dean

What are Thinkologie Books?

We believe in teaching language via stories. Stories bring cultural context and display regional differences as well.

Each story will be in English as well as the target foreign language. Each storybook will have an interactive book to test comprehension. The books will be in Kindle and Paperback.

This activity book is a workbook
created to go with the Kindle
version of the story.
Some 'bold' words are translated
into Hindi.
Write the answers in Hindi.
Find additional bilingual books on
our author page
https://www.amazon.com/author/
thinkologiebooks

Brainstorming Activity

Guess what the story is about by looking at the title and pictures.

Write or draw out a brief answer.

____

____

____

____

A quick search खोज with the words, 'Lata Mangeshkar' displays results mostly of her music संगीत. But her fan base is so huge and dedicated समर्पित that there are even journals called, "Don't Disturb Me When I am Listening to Lata Mangeshkar".

In 2022 India lost their beloved nightingale. Lata Mangeshkar was the recipient प्राप्तकर्ता of the highest civilian honors नागरिक सम्मान – Bharat Ratna, Padma Vibhushan, Padma Bhushan, and Dadasaheb Phalke awards. She was 92 years old.

The Early Years

Lata sang a raaga from Hindol for a room full of teachers शिक्षकों की when she was four or five years old, providing the educators शिक्षक a glimpse of her future.

She learned Hindi in homeschool and spoke her native language देशी भाषा of Marathi. Education in a school was not possible संभव as her dad traveled with his theatre group रंगमंच समूह constantly.

Multi-Lingual Talent

She told Scroll, a newsmagazine that she is mostly self-taught. She speaks, Hindi, Marathi, Urdu, a little Punjabi, and also learned Sanskrit and Tamil. And has sung गाया in 36 languages including, Dutch, Russian, Fijian, and Swahili.

Her parents died early and she was forced to become a breadwinner कमानेवाला. She lived with relatives all her life and never married. But in her own words, she never felt lonely as she was surrounded घिरे by her extended family and was well protected.

Fame Came Courting

Lata rose to fame and became Bollywood's Nightingale. She was the voice to many reels. She stirred up patriotism देश प्रेम by singing Ae Mere Vatan Ke Log after India's defeat हार at the hands of China in 1962. Her music was also the soundtrack गीत संगीत to many iconic Hindi films, Bazar, Veer Zara, and Maine Pyar Kiya.

Her first break came when Ghulam Haider signed her to sing in Bollywood. The music producers संगीत निर्माता recognized the freshness in her voice as well as the classical Hindustani training. She sang memorable अविस्मरणीय songs in the films Pakeezah, Mughal E Azam, and Dastak.

Her brother, Hridayanath Mangeshkar composed devotional धार्मिक music, Dyaneshwari for her to sing as well – music that showed off her vocal range.

Her best work was showcased with Madan Mohan in songs like Lag Ja Gale and Jara Si Aahat and Mai Ri from the movie Dastak.

Keeping up with the Times

Things started to change in the Eighties in Bollywood and many young playback singers entered the scene with modern आधुनिक vocal styles. Still, even as she aged, the quality गुणवत्ता of her voice remained impeccable. Music directors like A.R.Rahman chose her from among many young, fresh, and trendy playback पार्श्व गायक singers. She sang, O Paalanhaare in the 2001 film, Lagaan. She was a familiar voice to many older generations पीढ़ी and so to insert her in a modern movie proved successful.

Legacy

Lata has left behind a massive legacy विरासत and a nation in mourning. There is an outpouring of genuine grief for this beautiful singer. Her music संगीत will last for generations to come.

Why?

Because it was the soundtrack to many of India's son's and daughters' lives.

Sorting Activity

Read the text. Find and place the words in the box

Nouns	Proper Nouns
Abstract Nouns	Collective Nouns
Definite article	Indefinite article

Sorting Activity

Read the text. Find and place the words in the box

Adverbs	Verbs

Adjectives	Prepositions

Punctuation	Superlatives

Mark the Text

Use the following strategies to mark the text.

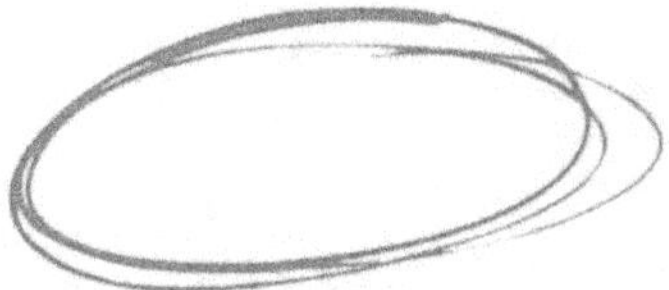

Circle content and look up the words in dictionary.com

Put a question mark near words that need explanation.

When did this story take place?

Where did this story take place?

What is the theme of this story?
e.g. love, slavery, war

FILL IN THE BLANKS WITH THE APPROPRIATE HINDI WORD

- A quick search________with the words, 'Lata Mangeshkar' displays results mostly of her music _________.

- Lata sang a raaga from Hindol for a room full of teachers ______when she was four or five years old.

- She learned Hindi in homeschool and spoke her native language ________of Marathi.

- And has sung ________in 36 languages including, Dutch, Russian, Fijian, and Swahili.

FILL IN THE BLANKS WITH THE APPROPRIATE HINDI WORD

- Her parents died early and she was forced to become a breadwinner __________.

- She stirred up patriotism _________ by singing Ae Mere Vatan Ke Log.

- The music producers __________ _________ recognized the freshness in her voice.

- She sang memorable __________________songs.

- Still, even as she aged, the quality __________of her voice remained impeccable.

FILL IN THE BLANKS WITH THE APPROPRIATE HINDI WORD

- She was a familiar voice to many older generations ____________.

- Lata has left behind a massive legacy __________ and a nation in mourning.

- Her music __________ will last for generations to come.

Do a Google Search and pick out the top ten songs of Lata Mangeshkar. Write out which movies they are from as well.

1.

2.

3.

4.

5.

Do a Google Search and pick out the top ten songs of Lata Mangeshkar. Write out which movies they are from as well.

6.

7.

8.

9.

10.

Create a One Pager

Draw and Label the Story

Write a Summary

What do you think about the story? Write
a few sentences.

Contact us

Our mission is to help other educators, coaches and homeschoolers also!

Contact us for customized interactive books. If you want to publish your book - contact us for that too!

Follow our author page

https://amazon.com/author/thinkologiebooks

We are also on Instagram @thinkologie

Twitter @ thinkologie

Facebook @thinkologiemedia